D0104876

Printed in the USA

A Message to Garcia

By Elbert Hubbard

Contents

APOLOGIA

HORSE SENSE

If you work for a man, in Heaven's name work for him. If he pays wages that supply you your bread and butter, work for him, speak well of him, think well of him, and stand by him, and stand by the institution he represents. I think if I worked for a man, I would work for him. I would not work for him a part of his time, but all of his time. I would give an undivided service or none.

If put to the pinch, an ounce of loyalty is worth a pound of cleverness. If you must vilify, condemn, and eternally disparage, why, resign your position, and when you are outside, damn to your heart's content. But, I pray you, so long as you are a part of an institution, do not condemn it. Not that you will injure the institution—not that—but when you disparage the concern of which you are a part, you disparage yourself. And don't forget—"I forgot" won't do in business.

This literary trifle, "A Message to Garcia," was written one evening after supper, in a single hour. It was on the Twenty-second of February, Eighteen Hundred Ninety-nine, Washington's Birthday, and we were just going to press with the March "Philistine." The thing leaped hot from my heart, written after a trying day, when I had been endeavoring to train some rather delinquent villagers to abjure the comatose state and get radio-active.

A trying day

The immediate suggestion, though, came from a little argument over the teacups, when my boy Bert suggested that Rowan was the real hero of the Cuban War. Rowan had gone alone and done the thing—carried the message to Garcia.

The real hero of the war

It came to me like a flash! Yes, the boy is right, the hero is the man who does his work—who carries the message to Garcia. I got up from the table, and wrote "A Message to Garcia." I thought so little of it that we ran it in the Magazine without a heading. The edition went out, and soon orders began to come for extra copies of the March "Philistine," a dozen, fifty, a hundred; and when the American News Company ordered a thousand, I asked one of my helpers which article it was that had stirred up the cosmic dust.

The increasing demand

"It's the stuff about Garcia," he said.

The next day a telegram came from George H. Daniels, of the New York Central Railroad, thus: "Give price on one hundred thousand Rowan article in pamphlet form—Empire State Express advertisement on back—also how soon can ship."

George H. Daniels

I replied giving price, and stated we could supply the pamphlets in two years. Our facilities were small and a hundred thousand booklets looked like an awful undertaking.

The result was that I gave Mr. Daniels permission to reprint the article in his own way. He issued it in booklet form in editions of half a million. Two or three of these half-million lots were sent out by Mr. Daniels, and in addition the article was reprinted in over two hundred magazines and newspapers. It has been translated into all written languages.

At the time Mr. Daniels was distributing the "Message to Garcia," Prince Hilakoff, Director of Russian Railways, was in this country. He was the guest of the New York Central, and made a tour of the country under the personal direction of Mr. Daniels. The Prince saw the little book and was interested in it, more because Mr. Daniels was putting it out in such big numbers, probably, than otherwise.

Prince Hilakoff

In any event, when he got home he had the matter translated into Russian, and a copy of the booklet given to every railroad employee in Russia.

The Russian railroad-men

Other countries then took it up, and from Russia it passed into Germany, France, Spain, Turkey, Hindustan and China. During the war between Russia and Japan, every Russian soldier who went to the front was given a copy of the "Message to Garcia."

The Japanese, finding the booklets in possession of the Russian prisoners, concluded that it must be a good thing, and accordingly translated it into Japanese.

The war in the East

And on an order of the Mikado, a copy was given to every man in the employ of the Japanese Government, soldier or civilian. Over forty million copies of "A Message to Garcia" have been printed.

This is said to be a larger circulation than any other literary venture has ever attained during the lifetime of the author, in all history—thanks to a series of lucky accidents!—E.H.

Its great circulation

A MESSAGE TO GARCIA

As the cold of snow in the time of harvest, so is a faithful messenger to them that send him: for he refresheth the soul of his masters.—*Proverbs xxv:* 13

In all this Cuban business there is one man stands out on the horizon of my memory like Mars at perihelion.

When war broke out between Spain and the United States, it was very necessary to communicate quickly with the leader of the Insurgents. Garcia was somewhere in the mountain fastnesses of Cuba—no one knew where. No mail or telegraph message could reach him. The President must secure his co-operation, and quickly. What to do!

I

The President needed a man

Some one said to the President, "There is a fellow by the name of Rowan will find Garcia for you, if anybody can."

And found one

Rowan was sent for and was given a letter to be delivered to Garcia. How "the fellow by the name of Rowan" took the letter, sealed it up in an oilskin pouch, strapped it over his heart, in four days landed by night off the coast of Cuba from an open boat, disappeared into the jungle, and in three weeks came out on the other side of the Island, having traversed a hostile country on foot, and delivered his letter to Garcia—are things I have no special desire now to tell in detail.

The point that I wish to make is this: McKinley gave Rowan a letter to be delivered to Garcia; Rowan took the letter and did not ask, "Where is he at?" By the Eternal! There is a man whose form should be cast in deathless bronze and the statue placed in every college of the land. It is not book-learning young men need, nor instruction about this and that, but a stiffening of the vertebrae which will cause them to be loyal to a trust, to act promptly, concentrate their energies: do the thing—"Carry a message to Garcia."

He delivered the message

General Garcia is dead now, but there are other Garcias.

The Moral

No man who has endeavored to carry out an enterprise where many hands were needed, but has been well-nigh appalled at times by the imbecility of the average man—the inability or unwillingness to concentrate on a thing and do it.

Slipshod assistance, foolish inattention, dowdy indifference, and half-hearted work seem the rule; and no man succeeds, unless by hook or crook or threat he forces or bribes other men to assist him; or mayhap, God in His goodness performs a miracle, and sends him an Angel of Light for an assistant.

You, reader, put this matter to a test: You are sitting now in your office—six clerks are within call. Summon any one and make this request: "Please look in the encyclopedia and make a brief memorandum for me concerning the life of Correggio."

There are other Garcias

Will the clerk quietly say, "Yes, sir," and go do the task?

On your life he will not. He will look at you out of a fishy eye and ask one or more of the following questions:

Who was he?

Which encyclopedia?

Where is the encyclopedia?

Was I hired for that?

Don't you mean Bismarck?

What's the matter with Charlie doing it?

Is he dead?

Is there any hurry?

Shall I bring you the book and let you look it up yourself?

What do you want to know for?

Which Encyclopedia?

What's the matter with Charlie doing it?

And I will lay you ten to one that after you have answered the questions, and explained how to find the information, and why you want it, the clerk will go off and get one of the other clerks to help him try to find Garcia—and then come back and tell you there is no such man.

Of course I may lose my bet, but according to the Law of Average I will not.

I wasn't hired for that anyway!

Now, if you are wise, you will not bother to explain to your "assistant" that Correggio is indexed under the C's, not in the K's, but you will smile very sweetly and say, "Never mind," and go look it up yourself.

And this incapacity for independent action, this moral stupidity, this infirmity of the will, this unwillingness to cheerfully catch hold and lift—these are the things that put pure Socialism so far into the future. If men will not act for themselves, what will they do when the benefit of their effort is for all?

A first mate with knotted club seems necessary; and the dread of getting "the bounce" Saturday night holds many a worker to his place.

Dread of getting "the bounce"

Advertise for a stenographer, and nine out of ten who apply can neither spell nor punctuate—and do not think it necessary to.

Can such a one write a letter to Garcia?

"You see that bookkeeper," said a foreman to me in a large factory.

"Yes; what about him?"

"Well, he's a fine accountant, but if I'd send him up-town on an errand, he might accomplish the errand all right, and on the other hand, might stop at four saloons on the way, and when he got to Main Street would forget what he had been sent for."

Who wants a man like this?

Can such a man be entrusted to carry a message to Garcia?

We have recently been hearing much maudlin sympathy expressed for the "downtrodden denizens of the sweat-shop" and the "homeless wanderer searching for honest employment," and with it all often go many hard words for the men in power.

Nothing is said about the employer who grows old before his time in a vain attempt to get frowsy ne'er-do-wells to do intelligent work; and his long, patient striving with "help" that does nothing but loaf when his back is turned. In every store and factory there is a constant weeding-out process going on. The employer is continually sending

9

away "help" that have shown their incapacity to further the interests of the business, and others are being taken on.

The weeding-out process

No matter how good times are, this sorting continues: only if times are hard and work is scarce, the sorting is done finer—but out and forever out the incompetent and unworthy go. It is the survival of the fittest. Self-interest prompts every employer to keep the best—those who can carry a message to Garcia.

This man says times are scarce

I know one man of really brilliant parts who has not the ability to manage a business of his own, and yet who is absolutely worthless to any one else, because he carries with him constantly the insane suspicion that his employer is oppressing, or intending to oppress, him.

He can not give orders; and he will not receive them. Should a message be given him to take to Garcia, his answer would probably be, "Take it yourself!"

Tonight this man walks the streets looking for work, the wind whistling through his threadbare coat. No one who knows him dare employ him, for he is a regular firebrand of discontent.

He is impervious to reason, and the only thing that can impress him is the toe of a thick-soled Number Nine boot.

A spiritual cripple

Of course I know that one so morally deformed is no less to be pitied than a physical cripple; but in our pitying let us drop a tear, too, for the men who are striving to carry on a great enterprise, whose working hours are not limited by the whistle, and whose hair is fast turning white through the struggle to hold in line dowdy indifference, slipshod imbecility, and the heartless ingratitude which, but for their enterprise, would be both hungry and homeless.

Have I put the matter too strongly? Possibly I have; but when all the world has gone a-slumming I wish to speak a word of sympathy for the man who succeeds—the man who, against great odds, has directed the efforts of others, and having succeeded, finds there's nothing in it: nothing but bare board and clothes. I have carried a dinner-pail and worked for day's wages, and I have also been an employer of labor, and I know there is something to be said on both sides.

There is no excellence, per se, in poverty; rags are no recommendation; and all employers are not rapacious and high-handed, any more than all poor men are virtuous.

A word of sympathy for the man who succeeds—

Rags not necessarily a recommendation

My heart goes out to the man who does his work when the "boss" is away, as well as when he is at home. And the man who, when given a letter for Garcia, quietly takes the missive, without asking any idiotic questions, and with no lurking intention of chucking it into the nearest sewer, or of doing aught else but deliver it, never gets "laid off," nor has to go on a strike for higher wages.

Civilization is one long, anxious search for just such individuals. Anything such a man asks shall be granted.

His kind is so rare that no employer can afford to let him go. He is wanted in every city, town and village—in every office, shop, store and factory.

Good men are always needed

Needed today and needed badly—

A MAN

The world cries out for such: he is needed, and needed badly—the man who can carry

A MESSAGE TO GARCIA.

17514385R00014

Made in the USA
Lexington, KY
18 September 2012